write

wr

I CAN WRITE!

A Book by

ME, MYSELF

with a little help from

Theo. LeSieg and *Roy McKie*

A Bright & Early Book
RANDOM HOUSE / NEW YORK

GROLIER
BOOK CLUB EDITION

I J K L M
6 7 8 9 0

1
2

fish in shoe

fish in

1

2

3

fish in tree

2

3

4

in the door

yellow

red

cow in bed

cow on chair

long red hair

blue

pink

cow in sink

5 jump rope

cow eats soap

orange

green

teeth are clean

6 bring clock

hole in sock

black

white

7 on kite

7

8

8 fish skate

8 9 10

Then

10 men

Oh boy

what a party

and

I

wrote

it

myself

I can

I can